The Unofficial Guide to
Engineering in
MINECRAFT®

SAM KEPPELER

PowerKiDS
press™

New York

Published in 2020 by The Rosen Publishing Group, Inc.
29 East 21st Street, New York, NY 10010

First Edition

Editor: Greg Roza
Book Design: Rachel Rising
Illustrator: Matias Lapegüe

Photo Credits: Cover, 1,3,4,6,8,10,12,14,16,18,20,22,23,24 (background) Evgeniy Dzyuba/Shutterstock.com; p. 5 peacefoo/Shutterstock.com; pp. 6,8,10,12,14,16,18,20 (insert) Levent Konuk/Shutterstock.com; p. 7 Lukasz Szwaj/Shutterstock.com; p. 8 (insert) mahirart/Shutterstock.com; p. 13 BigTunaOnline/Shutterstock.com; p. 22 StockLite/Shutterstock.com.

Library of Congress Cataloging-in-Publication Data

Names: Keppeler, Sam author. | Mojang AB (Firm) | Sony Computer Entertainment.
Title: The unofficial guide to engineering in Minecraft / Sam Keppeler.
Other titles: Engineering in Minecraft | Minecraft
Description: New York : PowerKids Press, [2020] | Series: STEM projects in
  Minecraft | Includes webography. | Includes index.
Identifiers: LCCN 2019016078| ISBN 9781725310506 (paperback) | ISBN
  9781725310520 (library bound) | ISBN 9781725310513 (6 pack)
Subjects: LCSH: Minecraft (Game)-Juvenile literature. | Human engineering. |
  Building-Juvenile literature. | Computer games-Juvenile literature. |
  Video games in education.
Classification: LCC GV1469.35.M535 K46 2020 | DDC 794.8/5-dc23
LC record available at https://lccn.loc.gov/2019016078

Manufactured in the United States of America

CPSIA Compliance Information: Batch #CWPK20. For Further Information contact Rosen Publishing, New York, New York at 1-800-237-9932.

Contents

Engineering a World

You can do a lot of things in the game of *Minecraft*. You can fight monsters. You can explore and find treasure and new **resources**. You can trade with villagers. And you can build structures of all shapes and sizes!

Minecraft doesn't have all the same rules of **physics** as the real world. This can help you build many unusual and interesting things. However, knowing how people **design** and create real things can also help you plan structures and features in the game—and it can teach you more about the principles of real-life engineering.

The first known engineer was Imhotep, who built the Step Pyramid in Saqqara, Egypt, about 2550 BC.

What Is Engineering?

Engineering is how people solve problems and design and build things using science and math. A person who specializes in engineering is called an engineer. If you design and build things in *Minecraft*, you're an engineer too!

There are many kinds of engineers. Civil engineers design public works such as buildings, roads, bridges, and harbors. They make sure these things are constructed in a safe, sturdy way. In *Minecraft*, think of building a base that enemies or **mobs** can't easily destroy or a road that connects your base and a village in the most direct fashion.

MINECRAFT MANIA

You can play *Minecraft* in a few different **modes**. In Survival mode, you have to find all your materials before you can build anything. In Creative mode, you already have all the blocks and materials you could want!

When you decide to build a base or a road in *Minecraft*, what do you do first? You have to pick a good site and make a plan.

Many Materials

Minecraft has many blocks of different **materials** you can build with. As an engineer, you have to choose the best ones for your structure. Think about what's important. If you're in Survival mode, you'll need your base to keep you safe. Some blocks are stronger than others. However, you also have to keep in mind how hard it will be to collect the blocks you need.

For example, it's often easy to collect dirt or sand in *Minecraft.* However, do these seem like the sturdiest materials? They're not! Obsidian is very tough—but it's much more difficult to collect.

<-- obsidian

MINECRAFT MANIA

Obsidian is a black block in *Minecraft* that's created when water hits a lava source block. That means it's mostly found deep underground. It can only be mined with a diamond pickaxe.

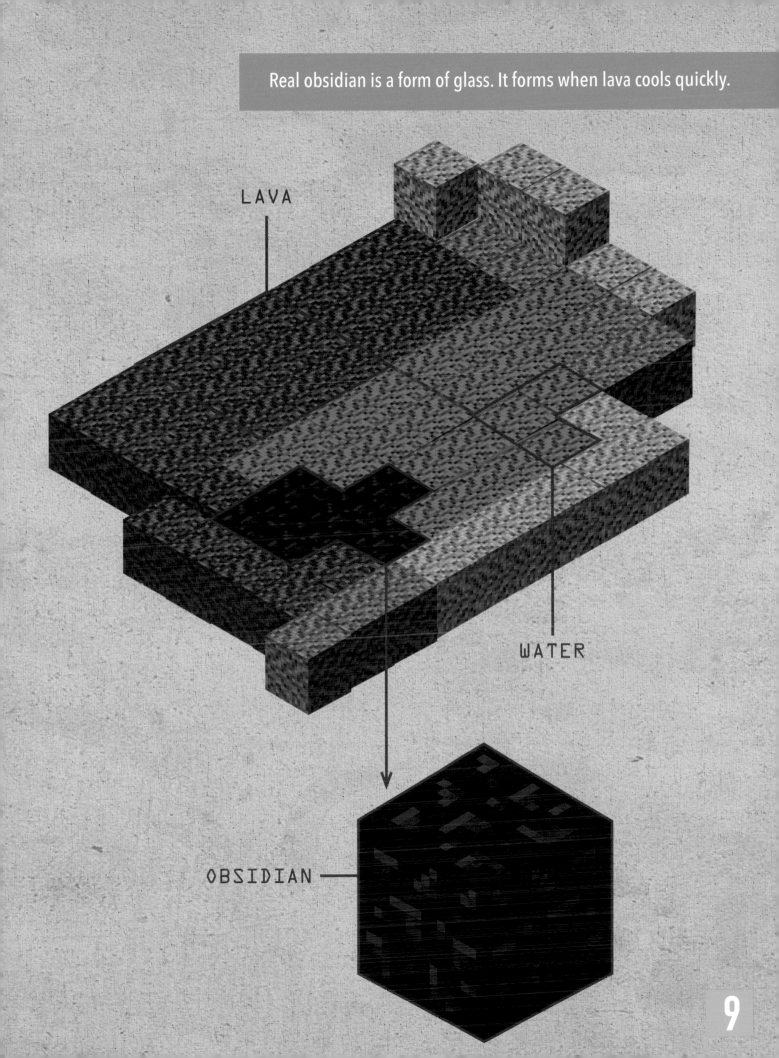

Real obsidian is a form of glass. It forms when lava cools quickly.

LAVA

WATER

OBSIDIAN

Make It Strong

It's important to think of **durability** when choosing materials for your building project. Blast resistance is how much damage a material can take from an **explosion**, such as one caused by a creeper or TNT. Obsidian has a blast resistance of 6,000. Most kinds of stone have a blast resistance of 30. Sand and dirt both have a blast resistance of 2.5. Glass only has a resistance of 1.5!

Some materials look nicer than others. *Minecraft* concrete comes in many colors. There are many patterns of **glazed** terra-cotta. However, these blocks have a low blast resistance. They may not be the best material for a strong castle.

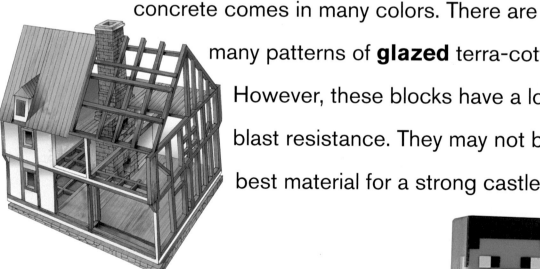

MINECRAFT MANIA

Some materials—including wood, wood **planks**, and wool—can burn when hit by lightning or exposed to fire or lava.

A *Minecraft* house built out of wood might be easy and look nice, but remember that wood can burn—and that wood planks only have a blast resistance of 15.

Big Plans

All engineers do some planning, but there are also engineers who specialize in making sure there are enough materials for a job and other planning concerns. When you're engineering in your *Minecraft* world, you need to think about these things too. Before you start a big build, make a plan. You can use that plan to figure out the amount of resources you'll need.

For example, say you want to build a house that's 10 blocks wide by 10 blocks deep. You want to use red concrete for the floor. How many blocks of red concrete will you need?

MINECRAFT MANIA

You can draw your plans for your *Minecraft* builds on graph paper, which has many lines making small, even squares on it. Since the basic **unit** of *Minecraft* is a block, this can keep things even and help you figure out how many blocks you need.

Plans for buildings or other constructions are called blueprints. They're often—but not always—created on blue paper.

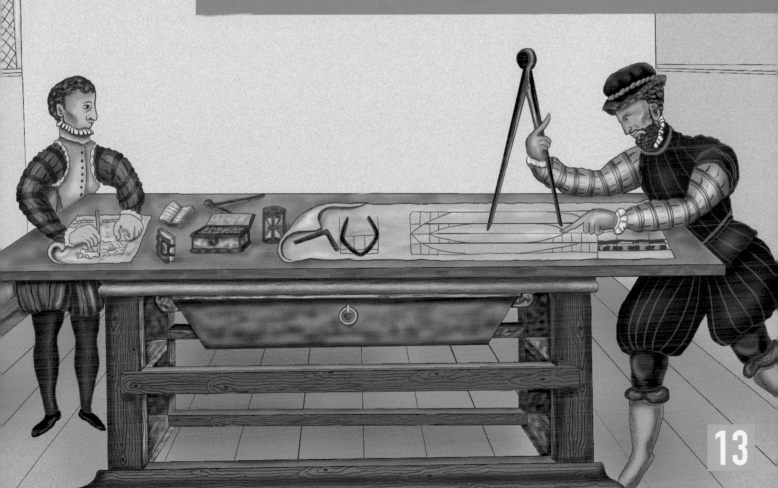

13

Firm Foundation

The first part of a structure you need to build is the foundation, or base. In the real world, engineers know a strong building needs a strong foundation to hold its weight. It supports the whole building and keeps it standing despite the pull of **gravity**. It also keeps water from weakening the building.

In *Minecraft*, gravity doesn't work the same way. Most blocks aren't affected by it. Still, your building will need a flat, stable base. A foundation also helps with planning because you can see what sort of a footprint your building will have on the land.

MINECRAFT MANIA

Most kinds of *Minecraft* stone have the same blast resistance (30), but you might think some kinds look better than others. You can make stone bricks by **smelting** cobblestone in a furnace and then combining four pieces of plain stone to make four stone bricks.

This foundation in a *Minecraft* world is made of stone bricks. Stone has a higher blast resistance than other building materials. Even if a creeper blows up part of your stone base, the foundation may remain, and you can rebuild.

On the Road

Engineering is used in building roads and highways, too. Civil engineers plan out the best routes for people to get from one place to another. They make sure the right materials are used for the road's surface. They also think about how to make roads go through land that isn't ideal, such as swamps and hilly areas.

There are no cars or trucks in *Minecraft*, but there are minecarts and horses you can ride. There are different concerns when planning a road for either one of them, or even when planning a path for walking from one site to another.

MINECRAFT MANIA

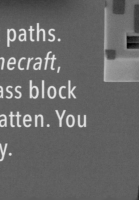

The first roads in history were dirt paths. You can make simple paths in *Minecraft*, too. All you need to do is tap a grass block with a shovel and the grass will flatten. You can use this trick to mark your way.

How would you plan a road through this *Minecraft* swamp? Swamps are often flooded and have many small islands.

The surface doesn't matter as much for a *Minecraft* road. Planning is more important. A *Minecraft* player can only jump a little more than a block at a time. Horses can jump varying distances, but you can't ride them through water deeper than two blocks.

When you're planning a road, think about how wide you want your route to be and how much you need to level any hills. Where will you need bridges? You can also build tunnels but remember that a player on a horse also needs more room to go under obstacles than a player does.

MINECRAFT MANIA

For minecart routes, you have to put down rails. It's good to have a route planned out that goes up or down gradually. You'll need powered rails (and a power source such as a redstone torch) to get your minecart to go up hills.

This tunnel goes through a hill in *Minecraft*. If you dig a tunnel, make sure that the tunnel is well lit to keep monsters from spawning. And be careful while digging—gravel and sand can fall on you!

Arches and Bridges

You can build amazing bridges for your roads in *Minecraft* because you don't have to worry about gravity with most blocks. Real-life engineers put a lot of work into bridges. You can too, but you don't have to worry about all the possible problems they do.

That's true with a lot of *Minecraft* builds. Although it's fun and helpful to consider engineering principles when playing and building, you don't always have to worry about real-life physics. Still, if you pay attention to the basic ideas, you can engineer some really awesome builds that can help you out and fit right in with the real world!

MINECRAFT MANIA

People have built with arches for years because they support a lot of weight. The supports carry the weight of the stones. In *Minecraft*, that weight's not a problem—but they still look cool!

Real bridges must have strong supports to hold up the surface and a strong, steady surface between those supports. In *Minecraft*, you can build unusual bridges without any worries about strength and support.

Making Mods

You can make your *Minecraft* creations even more exciting with modifications, or mods. Using a computer program called ScriptCraft, you can create new blocks, change the way the game functions, and make your own games. Imagine what you could create! You could apply the principles of gravity to more *Minecraft* blocks and see what would happen. Or, you could create a special strong glass that won't break!

If you're interested in learning how to create mods in *Minecraft*, visit the website below. You'll find the information needed to get started with ScriptCraft and build your own *Minecraft* mods.

https://scriptcraftjs.org/

Glossary

design: To create the pattern or shape of something. Also, the pattern or shape of something.

durability: How much something can stay in good condition over a period of time.

explosion: A sudden release of energy that causes harm.

glazed: Given a shiny, smooth coating.

gravity: The force that pulls objects toward Earth's center.

material: Something from which something else can be made.

mob: A moving creature within *Minecraft*. Often used to mean one of the monsters that spawns, or appears, in *Minecraft* at night.

mode: A form of something that is different from other forms of the same thing.

physics: The study of matter, energy, force, and motion, and the relationship among them, also the properties and composition of something.

plank: A heavy, thick board of wood.

resource: Something that can be used.

smelt: To heat to separate metals.

unit: A particular amount of something that's used as a standard for counting, measuring, or building.

Index

B
blast resistance,
    10, 11, 14, 15
bridges, 6, 18, 20, 21

C
concrete, 10, 12

D
dirt, 8, 10
durability, 10

F
foundation, 14, 15

G
glass, 10, 22
gravity, 14, 20, 22

H
horse, 16, 18

L
lava, 8, 9, 10

M
minecart, 16, 18

O
obsidian, 8, 9, 10

R
roads, 6, 7, 16, 17,
    18, 20

S
sand, 8, 10, 19
stone, 10, 14, 15

T
tunnels, 18, 19

W
water, 8, 18
wood, 10, 11
wool, 10

Websites

Due to the changing nature of Internet links, PowerKids Press has developed
an online list of websites related to the subject of this book. This site is
updated regularly. Please use this link to access the list:
www.powerkidslinks.com/stemmc/engineering